The Ti:
When There Was
No Bible

Written by Sam Gipp

Illustrated by Claudia West

DayStar Publishing

PO Box 464 • Miamitown, Ohio 45041

MW01596594

Dedicated to

My Grandchildren

Copyright © 2011
by Dr. Samuel C. Gipp

1st Printing July 2011

ISBN # 978-1-890120-70-2

The Jewish Bible, the thirty-nine books we call the Old Testment, was finished around 398 B.C. (that means **B**efore **C**hrist was born) with the book of the Prophet Malachi.

The last words God wrote to man were Malachi 4:5,6.

Behold, I will send you Elijah the prophet before the coming of the great and dreadful day of the LORD:
And he shall turn the heart of the fathers to the children, and the heart of the children to their fathers, lest I come and smite the earth with a curse.

Then, for the next four hundred years...

...God was silent.

397 B.C.

BETHLEHEM

1 B.C.

3

Then Jesus was born of a virgin in Bethlehem.

Few people realized at the time that this baby, Jesus, was the Lord's anointed One, or Christ.

Jesus did many wonderful things during his next thirty-three years on earth.

He healed,

He cast out demons,

He raised the dead,

and did many other miracles...

...and then...

...He was crucified to pay for our sins.

But three days and three nights later, He rose from the dead!

For the next forty days, He walked the earth and instructed His Disciples. Then He returned to Heaven. But not until He told His Disciples...

"All Power is given unto me in heaven and in earth. Go ye therefore, and teach all nations, baptizing them in the name of the Father and of the Son, and of the Holy Ghost: Teaching them to observe all things whatsoever I have commanded you: and, lo, I am with you always, even unto the end of the world. Amen."

That was in 33 A.D.

The Disciples began to proclaim His message everywhere they went.

But still, there were no new words sent from God to be written down.

11

Then, slowly, God opened the door of Heaven and began again to speak to men through the written word.

The first books in God's New Testament are called, The Gospels...

Matthew,
written in 37 A.D.

Mark, written in 57 A.D.

Luke, written in 63 A.D.

and John,
written in 90 A.D.

Next comes a book recording all that the Apostles, or followers of Jesus, did. It was written by Luke and is called The Acts of the Apostles. Some of the things it tells us about are...

The Lord's ascension into Heaven,

the coming of the Holy Spirit,

the Disciples preaching
to the multitudes,

the conversion of the
Apostle Paul,

Paul taking the
Gospel into Europe,

and Paul's arrest.

15

Then come the writings of the Apostle Paul, his letters to...

The Romans
Ephesians
1 & 2 Thessalonians
Philemon

1 & 2 Corinthians
Philippians
1 & 2 Timothy
and Hebrews.

Galatians
Colossians
Titus

Rome

Black Sea

Thessalonica

Philippi

GALATIA

Aegean
Sea

Colosse

Corinth

Ephesus

CRETE

Mediterranean Sea

Jerusalem

Red
Sea

Then God's New Testament has the letters of...

James

1 & 2 Peter

1, 2, 3 John

...and Jude.

Then it closes with the book of the Revelation which was written by John, the Apostle.

God had placed His New Testament Church in Antioch and was once again speaking to His people.

But down in Alexandria, Egypt, some very bad men by the name of Philo and Origen didn't believe the Bible, so they were cutting parts out of it as fast as they could.

Then they tried to get the Christians to use their "bible" instead of the right one from Antioch. But the Christians were too smart and would have no part of it.

Around 150 A.D., the Bible was translated from Greek into Latin and crossed into Europe where it was used to win millions of people to the Lord and to establish many churches.

This Bible was called the Old Latin, or Italic.

Meanwhile, the Roman Catholic Church had Origen's corrupted Alexandrian bible translated into Latin and tried to force God's people to use it instead of the Old Latin Bible from Antioch which they loved so much.

When they refused to use it, many of them were tortured and killed.

21

Then in 1516, a man by the name of Erasmus published the first Greek New Testament that had all the books in it as they had been used in Antioch.

But Greek wasn't a world language, and Latin had been taken over by the Catholic Church. God still didn't have His Bible in a language He could use to reach the whole earth. But up in England, He was working on it.

In England, God began to develop the English language. No one knew He would use this language to take His Gospel all around the world. But in 1604, the great King James I of England gathered the smartest men in his kingdom and told them to translate the Bible into English so that the common man could have his own copy to read. It was finished in 1611 and is called the King James Bible.

God then used it to establish churches all over the world. It was the Bible upon which the United States was founded in 1776.

This great country has sent missionaries all around the world, carrying the good news of the Gospel of Jesus Christ.

But the devil hadn't given up. Two men by the names of

Brooke Fosse Westcott

and Fenton John Anthony Hort said...

"We've found the real bible in Alexandria, Egypt. We should use it instead of that old King James." So they translated the bad Alexandrian bible into English and called it the Revised Version. Since then, it has been translated into English many times. Sometimes it is called the New American Standard Version, sometimes the Good News for Modern Man, sometimes the New International Version. But every time it failed to start even one little revival because God refused to bless it. God liked the King James Bible!

Today, many people hate the King James Bible.

But God's people love it and use it.

Today, many powerful men and Bible colleges are trying to get God's people to use these new versions. But if everyone throws out their King James Bibles and starts using the new bibles, we will again be at...

...the time when there was no Bible.

Let's use God's perfect word, the King James Bible!

OR,

we can use
the one pictured
on the next page.

Which one do YOU want?